Chef Omar Sagastume, has cooked all over the world.
His father was a Chef in his country of origin (Guatemala)

His father opens the very first Polo Campero in the country. Now, you will find a chain of these restaurants all over Central America, USA and Europe.

Chefs Omar's father, meat his mother working as a waitress in the same restaurant.

PICKING THE RIGHT CHEF
HANDS ON

BEING A CHEF EN LA COSINA

Cocky motherfuckers, yelling, screaming, working long hours, and having no life, that's the life of most Chef's.

Perfection and consistency, it's what most Chef's strive for, just to know that any little mistake in your kitchen, will be the chef's fault.

The dream of every Chef in the world is to have his name well recognized, perfection and consistency will be the only thing that will accomplish that goal, so when someone fucks up in our kitchen, we do not go easy on them.

As a chef I can tell you we could be hard on our help, but at the same time they are our family, we spend more time with all these people then the time we spend with our real families.

A good Chef has to be an inspiration to every cook in the kitchen, everyone looks up to you, everyone in your kitchen wants to be like you, most cooks are loyal to their Chef.

The SOU Chef, is the second in command, a good SOUChef is the second version of you, he will make sure the Chef's orders would be fallow to a T.

A Chef without a good SOUChef is nothing in his kitchen, the SOUChef is your other half in the kitchen, he is your best friend, your homeboy, your partner in crime.

As a Chef, I am very picky on places I go out to eat, I have seen a lot of shit being done in kitchens, most of it by a bunch of clowns that get up one morning and decide to call themselves CHEFS.

A lot of shit being done to the public and you have no idea when you go out to eat, dipping thin slices of pork overnight, with a little bit of vinegar, and sell it to you as Veal Parma on the next day is an old trick, you would pay four times the price and won't even know the difference, unless you are a trained Chef.

Creating fake   Filet Mignon, using leftover pieces of meat with a special glue from China, even butchers can't tell the difference, making you Chicken Croquettes with leftover Chicken fat and the guts of the chicken, the list can go on and on, so yes , I am extremely picky when I go out to eat.

The first thing I do, if I go out to eat, is to go to the bathroom, if the hygiene is good, most likely the kitchen is clean, check out their uniforms, are they clean? Some of the nastiest shit happens at the bar, right when order your drink, most of the soda machines, or beer dispensers, are only cleaned once a year, they have mold and all kinds of nasty shit, if you break it apart, the hose, the dispenser etc., you will not consume they beverage you just ordered.

I did a lot of consulting work as a chef, many different occasions I would find frozen food for up to a year, I found a frozen chicken over a year old in the freezer, when I asked the Chef if he would eat that, he said yes, I made him cook the chicken and made him eat it.

If you spec for someone to pay for a chicken that has been frozen for over a year, not only pay you for it, but expect him to come back, you are out of your freaking mind. It's calls common sense.

A lot of the rules in a good kitchen are simple and basic, don't cook anything you would not eat yourself, keep your kitchen clean, and cook fresh food.

Being in the restaurant business, it's one of the hardest things anyone can ever do.
It is kind of funny, when I see a couple talking about how romantic opening a restaurant would be. Trust me when I tell you, romance is the last thing on the list.

.

Nine out of 10 Chefs are divorced and there is a good reason for that.
Your expectations when you open a restaurant should be, never to have a weekend off again, to never spend time with your loved ones in the days they are off, you may get a Monday off if you lucky enough.

If your expecting to become rich after opening a restaurant, you are wrong, Chef's do make good money, but when you consider the amount of hours we put in, the money does not look that good after all, Chefs are not in-it for the money, it's the love and passion what drives us to be the best.

A lot of dysfunctional people working in restaurants, you have to have a very thick skin to work in that industry, people will tell you things the way they are, no bullshit around, straight up, like it or not, if you FOOD sucks, that is exactly what you would hear, YOUR FOOD SUCKS.

Not everyone has what it takes to be a Chef, I had kids working me, kids who went to CIA, J&W and come out to me with some bullshit excuse and say, Chef, I can't work Sundays, If someone said that to me, I made sure they work every Sunday straight for a whole year Thinking of becoming a Chef? Work in a restaurant for a good couple of years, see if that is really what you want to do for the rest of your life, save yourself 100k.

A lot of the lack of hygiene and problems usually happen in private own restaurants, the chain restaurants are cleaner and they follow the rules because they are corporate, they have to follow rules.

It takes a disciplined restaurant owner to follow the same rules, they do exist, though I have worked in private restaurants where the owner is just as disciplined as the Chef, it is beautiful when you find that combination, everyone on the same page.

The job as a Chef has changed since the 80s, back in those days the only thing we had to do was cook, that is no longer the case, we are responsible for the kitchen, inventory, scheduling, food cost etc.

Now these days you see a lot of PAPER CHEFS, those are the Chefs walking around with a clipboard telling everyone what to do, and you sometimes wonder if they really know how to cook.

We have the hands on Chefs, I like to think I belong to the hands on, the ones that are not afraid to get their hands dirty, we are the ones staying late with our crew, helping your dishwasher if you have to, helping the cleaning crew, the Old School type, first ones to go in and the last ones to get out.

People have lot more respect for the hands-on Chefs, we earn the respect of everyone, we are constantly teaching everyone new things and how to be better at what they do.

The job as a Chef is pretty much the same way all over the world, the only thing that changes is the pay.

The best thing a young Chef should do, is to travel the world, getting that first-hand experience it's crucial

Cooking is love, and understanding a culture, I can tell a lot about a person based on what that person eats.
Cooking is something you will not learn from a book, cooking is an expression of love, friendship and welcoming, that's why in many cultures the first thing they do is to offer you food as a sign of friendship.

I remember the smells coming out of my grandmother's kitchen, the expression on her face when she saw us eat, cooking is everything to me, I consider myself lucky to do something for a living that I love to do, being in a kitchen is never work for me, it's a pleasure. If I am stressed, or I want to unplug from the world, I go to my kitchen.

It's sad to see so many fast food establishments now these days, serving so much garbage, such entities are there to protect us and they are doing a horrible job. Seeing FDA on a package does not mean is always good for you.

Places like Chile and Argentina stared opening healthy fast food places, that to me SOUnds like a great idea, I hope it catches up with the rest of the world.

It's hard to understand why eating healthy can be so expensive in the US, it's almost a luxury to eat organic, if third world countries can sell cheap organic, why can't we? May be because big Pharma will not allow it, there is no money and no big profits keeping a country healthy.

80 percent of the people in the US has no idea how to cook, we need to change that, for our own good.

Heating things in a microwave all the time is not safe for us.
When I was a kid I rarely heard about cancer, it was something unusual, something you never heard. Now hearing about someone having cancer is no big deal, when did that become acceptable to us? And why.

I remembered when I was a kid, if you left a piece of bread out, that bread was no good the next day, had mold all over the place.

You leave a slice of white bread out now, and it will be good for 45 days, that cannot be healthy to anyone, if you put margarine outside, not even flies will get close to it, margarine is only one molecule away from being plastic, and is FDA approved, I have to question their values approving something like that.

BEING ON TOP OF YOUR CAREER AS A CHEF

  Owning restaurants, having your own catering business and your own coffee shops it's awesome, it's being on top of the world.

I owed Cardoos Gourmet Catering in Boston Mass.
Catering is the ultimate dream for every Chef, and the number one reason for it, you customize menus all the time, every function is different, every menu is different, every site is different, it does not get any better than that, it's the ultimate challenge for every Chef.

Dong off premises catering, you will not have control of the weather, if you smart and have the time, go and check the site on which you will cook the following day, the equipment can represent a problem at any time, if you are catering a BBQ and the grill does not turn on, you are in deep shit, if your convection oven does not work, you will be in deep shit as well, catering is the ultimate dose of excitement, a natural high, a do or die type of situation, everything has to be perfectly timed, if something goes wrong, you will have a domino effect and everything will collapse and you will be looking at a law sue on your hands, fucking up someone's special day is not something you want in your resume or be knowing for.

I wish I had the time or the money to do a reality show, behind the scenes of a catering event, you will have a heart attack watching. I hear some horror stories from other caterers.

I had eight box trucks and around 48 employees at my pick, making mistakes is human, catering a wedding event at Harvard in a boat, and having your Sue Chef telling you in the middle of the event, Chef I can't find the wedding cake anywhere, I think we left it at the shop, is not something you can take lightly, I told my Sue Chef I was going to extend the time of happy hour and dinner and by the dime of dessert, if he was not here with a wedding cake I was going to personally cut his balls off. I have no idea how he did it but he did it, at the end of the day we can go out, have a beer and laugh about all this crazy shit.

Having a good reputation is every Chefs dream, being well established will allow you to cater for a lot of high-end clients. I had all the best of the best in Boston Mass, Beacon Hill, New St, Wellesley Mass etc., with high end clients, celebrities will follow, I done work for Dick Cheney, Cheer, Rolling-stones, Celtics, Red Sox, Sting, Governors etc.

Getting to that point in your career takes a lot of work, it was not easy, just like everything in life, having determination it's what makes the difference between achieving your goal, I know a lot of people that tells me, god I wish I knew a different language, I wish I could travel more, I so want my Masters, wanting things does nothing to achieve your goal, it actually requires a lot of work and dedication, what is most important in life is to, first, know what you want, secondly make a plan and follow that plan, most people in the world want things, and they complain, and cry and blame everyone and everything but themselves.

 As a kid I knew what I wanted, I did not have the luxury to waste any time, I had a good vision from the very beginning.

Margie Kaithz

Restaurants make good money, but the real money is in Catering, I had clients such as BC, they called me for all the events, up to five thousand people, I had Margie Kaithz from National Lumber, she always had large events for her employees, she was very nice to her employees, every year, she will do a big Lobster Baked for all the employees, I remember bringing up to 20 Fryolator and filled them with water instead of oil, and use them as boiling hot water pots for the lobsters, she always had a minimum of two thousand people on her events, not to mention the holiday parties.
Her favorite food is Lobster

Earni Boch Jr
He was always doing private events, he loves his music, I catered at his private hanger many

times while having Rock and Roll bands playing there.
We did a lot of catering at this car dealerships, every-time he unveiled a new Ferrari or a new Maserati we were there to cater the event.
All of the events at his private home were catered by us, his favorite food was the one at the end of the year, the holidays, especially Thanksgiving.

Mick Jagger from the Rolling Stones

Ronnie Woods, loves to paint, the man loves art, so I cater a lot of events for him at the Newbury St gallery, on which Mr. Mick Jagger would attend every single time.

Mick Jagger loves Vodka and loves to eat his Sushi. I had the pleasure of cooking for him a couple of times, great people, great guys.

The singer Cher

She loves her Kosher chicken SOUp, every single time she went to Boston, she would call and order her Chicken SOUp, she also order other items on the menu, but I know she loves her SOUp, she went to the trouble of calling me personally to let me know how good her SOUp was.

Denny DeVito and his wife Rhea Pearlam

They love their Meat Knishes, good Pastrami and a good Roast Beef, I was the Executive Chef in a Jewish restaurant in Brooklyn Mass, they used to go out to eat there on the weekends.

Both of them are really nice people, just normal people like everyone else out eating with the family.

The list goes on and on, it is nice to know and meet a lot of celebrities and find out that they are really nice people, everything you spec them to be. Every now and then you will meet someone who is not so nice, I prefer to reserve the names, but they out there, pretending to be nice and smiling for the cameras.

Once you accomplish or become a big shot Chef, the money follows, the only problem is that you never have time to spend it, always working, and one day when you are not working you are way too tired to enjoy anything.

I had a boat, I was lucky enough if I took that boat out on the water a couple of times a year, I did get to enjoy my motorcycle a lot, I will ride to work.

The first day my pool was ready I was too tired to go in, again, I did get to enjoy my jacuzzi a lot, it was relaxing after hards day work, just to be inside that hot water was heaven.

People often said, you have to find a balance in life, for Chefs that's not even a choice, if you get a job as an Executive Chef anywhere and you decide to work only 40 hrs a week, you would be fired in a week.
A lot of the good Chefs and after hearing so much about their wives, about never being at home, take jobs as corporate Chef and become miserable, I myself, after hearing my ex wife complain about me not being home , I took a job in Emerson Hospital, in charge of the nutrition department.
I had to wear a tie and I was not even allowed to cook, when you take jobs like that, you give away your creativity, you give away who you are and become nothing but a robot.

When you become a Chef in demand, work never stops, that's when I built a new home, when I bought my toys, the pool, jacuzzi etc and around the same time it's when my wife asked me for a divorce.

It sucks, after so much work, and you family make it all the way to the top, and your reward is to have your family walks away from you.

I met my wife in the business, so I never thought that would happen to me, I would say in my head, she understands, she was one of my waitresses for Christ sake, I was very wrong. It hard to meet a married Chef.

Very successful Chefs are divorced, due to the amount of time you spend in your kitchen.
My father was a Chef, that's how he met my mother, she was a waitress. They worked in Pollo Campero in Guatemala City.

As a Chef on top of your game, you can be a lot more creative and your clients will accept your creativity a lot easier, we can come up with really exotic dishes such as, alligator sushi, bear mini sliders, etc.

That's the best thing about being a Chef, creativity has no limits, yes a lot of people go to school to become a Chef, but to become a really go Chef, it's a gift, you have to have in you, it's an art, it's a form of expression, some people thinks they have that gift and that's just not the case in a lot of kitchens.

If you watched Kitchen Nightmares, you can see exactly what I am talking about. I remember Chef Ramsey ordered a salad in one of the episodes, and the Chef in the kitchen fried the lettuce, wtf, that's not being creative, that's just being plain stupid, so as I said, it's a gift, the gift to know how something is going to taste before you even make it, the gift to mix different ingredients and come up with a perfect dish.

Ingredients to become a good Chef:

Discipline

Determination

Consistency

Dedication

And love for what you do

I never care about how much money I was going to make when I started cooking, for most of us, money has nothing to do, we do it from the bottom of our hearts.
We are part of a lot of special days for people, part of so many weddings, birthdays, quinceaneras, and that alone makes our job awesome, I married a lot of my friends, and a lot of people still calls me for their anniversaries

I used to tease a friend of mine, he was a baker, a lot of people think that Chef and Bakers is the same thing, far from that.
Bakers have to be very precise, it's more chemical and Chefs have to trust their creativity.

So I teased my friend all the time, how in the world do you charge 2k for water and flour, you are a thief, of course I was only kidding, yes it was flour and water, but the time he spent making that cake was what mattered, he was a master, always on top of his game.

Chef's work a little different, we see a few ingredients and a thousand recipes go inside our heads immediately.

I was also the proud owner of Cafe Mayan, located in North Grafton, Mass, I was importing coffee from my family in Guatemala City, it was a small cafe, very upscale type of place, it had a mirror Italian painting on the wall, cozy, romantic, exotic, we had live music every Friday night, jazz was our favorite.

The cafe had hand crafted sandwiches, exotic things on the menu, turkey cranberry wrap, filled with homemade stuffing and sweet roasted apricots.

We were delivering to a lot of businesses around the area, we had a couple of colleges nearby, so the cafe was filled with college students all the time, my goal was to make that a franchise, I wanted to open six of them, unfortunately, due to personal issues it was not possible to make that dream happened at the time. Wrong timing, that's all.

We used to have these little fancy black lunch boxes, with a wrap, a homemade cookie, gourmet potato chips, our crafted water bottle, the idea was to be different from the rest, to be classy, to make our clients feel special, and we did make our people feel special, a lot of people called us and thanking us for the great service, and to tell us how wonderful the food was, that is the best pay check any Chef can receive every week, to hear how happy your clients are, that is all we want, that's the ultimate goal.

It's different when you go to chain restaurants, I am not going to speak for all of them of course, but most of them do work for a paycheck, and that's a big problem for a client, when you do something just for money, there is no pride inside, no motivation, no love.

It's nice when you go to a place and the Chef comes out and says hi to you, when the Chef comes out after your meal, and ask you if everything was good, those types of places are good, they care for you, they care about your opinion, and when someone care that much about you, that's definitely the place that you may want to consider becoming a regular.

Romey's Gourmet
That was my little Bistro, also located in North Grafton, this was the kind of place where we had gourmet items ready cooked and good to go.

If you were the busy type, my place was perfect for you, swing by after work and pick up a nice gourmet dinner ready to go, a maple glazed roasted duck, some basmati rice and may be a little sweet roasted caramelized squash, great items and great prices.

We had the police station next to us, we did a lot of catering for them as well, we had reservation only Friday night dinners, if you did not have a reservation it was impossible to sit you down due to the size of the place, it was just a small bistro, live music every Friday night.

To me class has always been important, class is something you cannot buy, you can be broke, no money, but you can still be one classy son of a bitch, I see people with money all the time with absolutely no class, what a shame.

In every place I owed, I made sure I had that special touch of class, even when we did a catering job, we made sure we decorated properly to the occasion.

Everything is important in every occasion, the music, photographer, flowers etc., but the food, everyone will always remember the food, for the simple fact that food represents love, if the food was not good or up to standards, trust me when I tell you, people will talk about that for many years to come.

Picking up the right caterer its important, a few tips in order to do that, always ask for a sample dinner, have the Chef go to your house and make sure he or she cooks for you, make sure you like the food and make sure you have a special connection with your Chef as well, again and again I will keep telling you, food is love, there for you need to have that connection with your Chef.

I had a good friend, he was and outstanding Chef, but he always asked why I made more money than him, he asked me one day to be completely honest with him, as a Chef we have no problem being honest with one another, so I told him, you are an asshole, your food is great, but people don't like you, stop being so Aragon all the time connect with people, be part of their of their celebration, as I said, that connection with your Chef is very important.

In every single place I owed, talking to my clients and getting to know them before I did the job, was crucial for me.

Many of my clients came to my shop thinking they knew what they wanted, you have to remember, this is what we do for a living, it's important you listen to your Chef, this is why you are hiring a professional, what good is it to hire a good lawyer if I am not going to take his advice, it's the same thing for us, make sure your Chef checks the site of the event ahead of time, make sure he cooks for you before your event, if a Chef does not do that, and he is quick on taking your money, without asking questions, may be that is not the right Chef for your event.

On your special day things will only happen one time, there is no rewind button, so be very careful picking the right people to execute the job.

Never pay the full amount ahead of time, always try to leave 50 percent to pay the day before the event.

Check references, ask around, see the credibility of his company.

We were in the preferred caterers list of some of the best venues in Mass, that's important as well, see how many venues they cater at, you can't just take someone's word now these days, that's part of your homework, it is the most important quest you have to face when getting ready for your special day, choosing the right people to get the job done.

As a Chef I always recorded the event, and I would advise that the clients do the same thing, videos and pictures are hard to deny, they tell the truth most of the time, if something does not go well, you will have all the proof you need right in your hands, everything had to go according to your contract, step by step, timing is everything when doing a catering job, it's what made me one of the best caterers in the state, timing is everything.

A good Chef will always be a couple hours ahead of time on site, before your event, seeing a Chef running around like a chicken with his head cut off, it's usually not a good sign. A good Chef will always be come and have everything under control at all times.

As I mentioned already, having a good relationship with your clients is everything, I took it to a very personal level all the time. I would send them birthday cards, happy anniversary cards, holidays, etc., I was always there all year round, so it was kind of hard for you not to think of me whenever you have an event coming up.

As a matter of fact, I practice that same method in all of my business, to take it to a personal level, I like to think of my clients as personal friends, people that I would do anything to help them in case they need me.

Yes, everyone has a business to make money, and money of course it's important, but if you take whatever business you have to that personal level, money will follow eventually.

The best clients I had were the ones when money was not an issue, that's every Chef's dream, it allows you to be very creative, I did a Fenway park event one time, we did a replica of Fenway Park, we even had the Green Monster, I think the whole event came to 97k altogether, it was a piece of art.

As a Chef, you will also be challenged with low budget jobs, those jobs are hard, but our job is to help them as well, as I said before, you don't need money in order to be classy, little bit of extra work, but it can be done.

Most people are under the idea that all the money is on the food, I had people tell me all the time, Chef, what if I don't have 150 guest and I have 140, how much would that be/. Honestly, you can go down to 100 guests, and it will not make a difference on the price, the money is never on the food, the money will always be on labor, that is where most of your money goes all the time, labor.

Chefs work very hard, in between all businesses, I went   a whole year and a half without a day off, it takes a toll on the family, it's really hard, but that's the job we choose to do, and as I said, to us is not a Job, is who we are.

PLACES I COOKED

México

Costa Rica

Guatemala

Belice

Jordán

Miami

Boston

NY

These are just some of the places I had the pleasure of cooking, it is interesting when you travel, cooking is not just about food, cooking is an understanding of a culture, and when you are lucky enough to travel to those places, share meals with the locals and spend time with them, you will understand their food a little better.

MEXICO

We have a big misunderstanding on different cuisines all over the world, for some reason a lot of people in the US thinks they know what Mexican food is.

If I would open a real Mexican place in the US, people may think I am cooking French, imagine a real Mexican place with Sopes, Tortas, Mole,

Chilaquiles, Esquites, Chilies rellenos, Picadillo, god I can go on and on as my mouth waters as I write.

Traveling is a must for every Chef, to understand a culture 100%, food itself is a language on its own.

I have had the pleasure to work and lived in Mexico for a few years, food means a lot to Mexican people, food is everything to them, it's how they show their love, their friendship, it's how they will welcome you to their house.

Breakfast in Mexico is very different from the US, actually I do miss Breakfast in the US, Mexican are not big lovers of eggs, a typical breakfast in Mexico contains a lot of protein, chicken stew, beef stew, pollo guisado, rice, beans, tortillas, SOUp. It's actually a good SOUrce of food to start your day.

Breakfast in Mexico is heavy, as much as I love breakfast food in the states, a Mexican breakfast has more benefits for my body for the out-coming day.

Lunch, it is typical to eat tortas (Mexican version of a panini) there are many versions of tortas, chorizo with avocado, Mexican Oaxaca cheese and shredded pork (awesome) they have the carnitas torta, pork cooked in its own fat, slowly, I guess is their version of a pork confit, SOUps, caldo de res, the beef is cooked slowly until the bone marrow comes out, it has carrots, cabbage, potatoes, it's delicious.

Mole, Mexico has 32 states, every state has their own version of Mole, if you are in Puebla and you are from Monterrey and you eating Mole, you better not say your Mole is the best, they take that very serious.

The amazing thing about Mole is the amount of ingredients that it has, it is one of the unique recipes in the world with the most amount of ingredients, besides from Indian cuisine of course.

Tortillas, Mexico has so many versions of tortilla thanks to the variety of corn they have, they have black tortillas, purple tortillas, yellow ones, it's amazing the variety of tortillas they have.

Chilaquiles, the Americans took it and call them Nachos, but in Mexico, chilaquiles is something you eat for breakfast, crispy chips, topped with a warm tomato sauce, sprinkled with fresh cheese and a couple of eggs over easy.

Taco Bell is a fantasy Mexican food, there is no Taco Bell in Mexico, it's just not Mexican food, and some of the names are pathetic such as, churrito, who comes up with those names anyway, that means little dick in Spanish, chalupa? What that fuck those that even mean? All of that food is overloaded with cheese, Mexicans do not eat that much cheese.

I often wonder how does that even happen? A complete misunderstanding of whole countries cuisine, is it lack of people not traveling? But even if that is the case, there is the internet, now these days it's hard to be ignorant, we have all the tools to find out.

It's an insult to a whole country to have something like Taco Bell, a complete misrepresentation of a whole country and culture.

Let me tell you something really hilarious? Chicken Milanese, it's very popular in Mexican cuisine.

And Italian dish in every Mexican restaurant, you can order a Chicken Milanese with tortillas, some beans and rice it is not uncommon in Mexico, I find that to be hilarious. The Italians would have a heart attack, if they knew that.

The Mexican cuisine is different in every state, same recipes with different versions of it, very interesting for a Chef.

Of course you will find other restaurants in Mexico, it is a country with 120 million citizens, so they have a good variety of restaurants, great sushi places, nice steak houses and a lot of international food, especially if you are in the city, the city is huge, if you are in Mexico City it's like being in NY, options everywhere, lots of Italian places as well.

One of my favorite restaurants in Mexico, is one of the steak houses, they have a huge buffet for your sides, and those sides include shrimp, clams, salads etc., when you go back to your table, there is a variety of waiters coming to your table, each one of them will have a big steal with a different cut of meat with them, it is great, one of them would come with chorizo, the other one would come with prime rib, another one with filet mignon, it's just crazy, Mexicans consider that type of restaurant expensive, it is a barging if you are an American, all that for 500 pesos, around 30USD per person.

I urge you to come and dine in Mexico, you will have one of the best experiences in your lifetime.

A tip, most people will tell you that you do not tip in Latin America, due to the fact that they work for their salary, not true, you always tip at least 10% while being in Mexico and if the service was excellent, which it usually is, you tip a little more, it is the right thing to do.

I learned so much about Mexican cuisine in my time being here, and I still have so much more to see I am sure, Mexico is a very unique place to be, it's a world on its own.

The beaches are amazing, the colonial towns are gorgeous and the people are always so friendly, and very welcoming.

GUATEMALA

Oh, my gorgeous Guatemala, land of the Mayans, land of a lot of history, right in the heart of Centro America, being right next to

Mexico you would think the food is just like Mexico, wrong, very different styles of cooking.

The city has about one million people, it's a small city, compared to other places, Guatemala has gorgeous places to visit, Lake Atitlan, Antigua Guatemala, Peten, Playa Blanca etc.

Guatemala is border with Belize, Mexico, Salvador, Honduras, that's a lot of borders for a small country.

The nickname for Guatemalans is CHAPINES, Chapin is a little rooster, the shorter rooster there is, Guatemala means Land of the trees in Mayan.

Guatemala is well known for coffee, everywhere in the world that you go, you will see their coffee, it is excellent, it has a lot to do with all the minerals in the ground, it makes it unique, Guatemala had 8 regions of coffee, each one of them with different unique minerals for coffee, and the altitude for the coffee it is just perfect.

Dunkin Donuts or Honey Dew do not exist in Guatemala, it would be and insult to what they do, it also would be impossible for you to order and iced coffee down there, that would be as if you ordered a bottle of good scotch and add water to it, it makes absolutely no sense whatsoever.

Guatemala also produces one of the best rums in the world, Zacapa, is well known all over the world, their pride and joy.

The zone of Zacapa is near where my family is from, a lot going on in that part of the country.

The food, their typical dish, Churrasco Chapin, again, every state has their own version of it, Guatemala has 22 states, a Churrasco will have a piece of prime rib grilled served with a couple of longanizas (their own version of chorizo) refried black beans, a delicious guacamole, rice pilaf and of course, tortillas, it is an amazing dish, you feel like going to siesta time right after a meal that big, and yes, siesta time over there is a common thing to do.

Guatemala's take their lunch time seriously, they do not like being interrupted while they are eating, you do not knock in someone's house when they are eating, businesses close, so they can eat in peace and quiet.

A good stew of black beans with pork bones and hard boil eggs is common down there, it is served with warm tortillas, steaming hot.

They have the flautas, it is a delicious taco, rolled and deep fried, topped with cheese and a red or green salsa.

Caldo de Mariscos, to die for, it's a seafood stew, again, depending on the state you are, the recipe is different, lobster, fish, crabs, shrimp, clams all in to a red tomato stew, with some potatoes and a little rice, and of course, hot tortillas, a nice cold beer.

Chicharones after roasting the pork for hours, its fry after roasting, it is just heaven, with some tortillas and squeeze a little lemon and salt and you are good to go.

Drinks like horchata, it is a drink made out of rice, amazing and refreshing on a hot day, Guatemala, just like the rest of Latin countries, they show their love with food, going to someone's house and say no to food is considered to be an insult.

When you sit down to eat and you finish your plate, the family asks you if you want more, if you say no thank you, they will put a little more on your plate, if you absolutely do not want anything else, you better have a loaded gun with you.

Sundays it is all about the family for Guatemalans, food, football and friends and church, it is a country rich with traditions.

In all my travels I always realized that the people that are quick to help you are the ones that have almost next to nothing, the people with no money are the ones to help you eat if you have no money, if you don't have a place to stay, they are the ones to offer you a bed, I can hint in the US that I am going to visit and no one would say come and stay here with us, if you stay in a hotel in a Latin country with friends there, it's an insult for them, I made that mistake once until my friend went to get me, a hotel? He says, why would stay in a hotel when you know you have a house here.

It is amazing how well they will treat you. Tamales, oh man, they have chicken tamales, beef tamales, Chuchitos which is like a mini tamale but on steroids, with a lot more flavor then the bigger one.

If you ever go to Guatemala, order the Churrasco Chapin, I think you will be more than satisfied, get on a diet before traveling down there and try everything, you will not regret it.

USA

I get very upset when people make fun of Americans for not having original cuisine.

People who say that the only thing we eat is hamburgers, pasta and pizza, they are full of shit, a lot of things to be proud in the USA.

I have been in many different countries around the world, and there is no Breakfast like the good old USA, we are the kings of breakfast.

Steak and eggs, home fries, we have some of the best steak houses around the world.

Like other countries we do have many states as well, everything is different in every state,

Boston for example, the clam chowder is amazing, you also have the Portuguese people up in Fall River, they are masters at cooking seafood.

New York, some of the best damn pizza in the world, that thin crust pizza, known all over the world.

I was in a remote island years ago (Monte Rico) and I ordered the pizza, I immediately recognized the style, I went to the kitchen and spoke the cook, he was an immigrant that worked in NY, and it was nice to see that he brought that style of cooking to his hometown.

Chicago, speaking of Pizzas, that's is the place for a deep dish, I love a good deep-dish pizza, seafood is my favorite, lots of shrimp, crab meat, topped with a white sauce, the best.

Florida
The best Cuban food is in Miami, Ropa Vieja, a good Cuban sandwich, a good guisado, forget about it.

San Francisco

The variety of food it's unbelievable in San Francisco, everything at a very reasonable price.

Texas

Meat, and more meat, Baby Back Ribs, briskets, oh yeah, I love Texas cuisine, no small portions in Texas, everything is big there.

California

We have a mix of everything there, due to the Hispanic population, the presence of Mexican food there is very strong, as well as the Central American food.

Louisiana

Jambalaya baby, oh yeah, spicy delicious, steaming hot, the French have a strong influence there.

They are masters at what they do.

The variety of food in the USA is outstanding, for someone to say we only eat burgers and pastas, I feel like slapping them across the face.

Georgia

Best fried chicken in the world, the SOUth has a lot to offer, it may not be the healthiest food on the planet, but I am sure as Hell, it will be damn delicious.

We are also blessed with some of the best chefs from all over the world.
Guys who made a name for himself and became famous.

Emerald Lagasse, Antony Bourdain, this guy are legends.

Oh yes, the good USA has a lot to offer, don't let anyone tell you different. A lot to be proud of.

Miami
Funky, upscale, fancy, it's what comes to mind if we talk about dining in Miami.

Yes, Miami could be a very expensive place to eat, but the nice thing about Miami is the variety of cuisine.

Chef's from all over the world and some of the best chefs from all over the USA gather in Miami to perform their best work.

It is amazing how creative the new generation of Chefs are now these days, and is also refreshing to see that the new generation of chefs are just as hungry as I was back in my day.

MIAMI's culturally diverse tastes permeate both high-end restaurants on SOUth Beach, as well as less expensive cafeterias and counters around the city. Here are some of Miami's most delectable multicultural dishes.

Ropa vieja

The Spanish name translates to "old clothes," referring to the way the beef is shredded and stewed in a tomato-based sauce. Though the meat used is the same as in vaca frita, the resulting dish is completely different.

Plantains

Maduros are plantains sliced and fried to make a sweet side dish that goes great with rice, beans, and any kind of meat. Another common way to enjoy plantains is twice-fried and salted as tostones — crunchy on the outside and soft inside.

Aja de gallina

Miami is also a great place for Peruvian food. The shredded chicken in this dish is in a creamy yellow sauce and served with white rice. It's unlike any chicken you've ever had before. You'll find it in most Peruvian restaurants in Miami, including the popular Happy Hour spot, Ceviche

Ceviche

Another traditionally Peruvian specialty, ceviche, is made of fresh fish marinated in citrus juices. The flavors of ceviche are unique, depending on the seafood chosen and the juices and spices used to marinate them. Coconut Grove restaurant Jaguar offers the perfect introduction to ceviche, with a variety of ceviche spoon samplers.

Palomilla steak

One of Miami's oldest and most important Cuban restaurants is Versailles on historic Calle Ocho. Here you'll find a lot of Cuban favorites for breakfast, lunch, and dinner. But the best dish of the bunch is the palmella steak, or the butterflied beefsteak. It's a thin steak, grilled to perfection, and served with French fries.

Churrasco

For a hearty piece of meat, try the churrasco, or grilled skirt steak. This cut of meat can be found at most Brazilian or Argentinian steakhouses and is often served with chimichurri, an oily sauce made with finely chopped green herbs. But for a twist on a classic, check out Finka's take. Their churrasco steak is served with truffle green beans on a bed of sweet potato mash, with a tangy Asian version of chimichurri.

Yuca

Yuca, also known as cassava, is a potato-like root vegetable that is almost as important as rice in Latin cuisine. It's typically prepared in two different ways: Boiled and served with a garlic sauce (known as mojo), or fried either in little bites or like thick-cut fries and served with a dipping sauce, like a creamy cilantro garlic sauce. Pollo Tropical has a great version.

Stone Crabs

SOUth Florida seafood is always fresh. Aside from ceviche, one particular seafood favorite in Miami is the Florida Stone Crab. And the best place to get your fill is at Joe's Stone Crab, where you can dig into fresh Stone Crab claws from October 15th to May 15th. The sweet claw meat can be dipped into melted butter or their famous mustard sauce. You can also get the Stone Crab Bisque or Crab Cakes from the menu.

Cinnamon Rolls

Another seasonal delight is Knauss Berry Farm's cinnamon rolls. The farm, where you can pick tomatoes and strawberries, is known best for its bakery, where you can get fresh pies, cookies, and their warm gooey cinnamon rolls. People wait in line for up to two hours for these mouthwatering rolls. To help the long wait, you can enjoy a thick, cold milkshake (the key lime one is particularly delicious). But if you want to avoid driving all the way to Homestead, Knauss Berry teams up from time to time with local smokehouse Miami Smokers, who bakes their cured bacon into the rolls. Knauss Berry closes up shop from mid-April until about November.

Churros and hot chocolate

If you're visiting on one of the two days of the year where the temperatures hover under 50 degrees, head over to La Palma to warm up. Churros are fried dough pastries covered in sugar and they pair flawlessly with a hot cup of cocoa. This is probably not the hot chocolate you're used to — it's thick and SOUpy, perfect for dipping.

SOUthern Cooking

Miami Beach's Yardbird is the perfect place for some great SOUthern comfort food and hospitality. Perfect for brunch, their signature dish is chicken and waffles which comes with a honey hot sauce. Save room for some of the small plates, like the mac and cheese, grits, biscuits, and the fried green tomato BLT. This is a great place to go with a big group and share.

The list can go on and on, and that is what makes Miami a great place to dine
The variety.

COSTA RICA

There are so many delicious dishes that are a must-try when visiting Costa Rica. Traditional Costa Rican food is definitely a blend of comfort food and grandma's home cooking with a flavor-bursting Latin flare. In Costa Rica, family-owned and operated small restaurants are called sodas. Sodas, which there are a countless number of throughout the country, is where you are likely to find some of the best varieties of traditional Costa Rican cuisine

Casado

A Casado – strangely translating as "married man" – is a typical plate of Costa Rican food. While there are all sorts of varieties of this plate, traditionally it includes rice and beans, salad, fried sweet plantains, and a protein – either fish, chicken, pork, or beef. Some Casado's will come with a slice of fresh cheese,

French fries or grilled vegetables. A Casado basically has all the staples of a perfectly balanced meal and is the comida tipica (typical food) of Costa Rica. This plate is served for lunch or dinner.

This was one of my favorite plates when I was in Costa Rica.

Gallo pinto

You cannot come to Costa Rica without having Gallo pinto at least once; though it is highly unlikely that you will be able to resist eating it more. Gallo pinto is traditionally served with breakfast, but can also be served later in the day. Gallo pinto is a slowly blended and married together dish of rice, beans, onions, red peppers, and cilantro. Gallo pinto served with eggs, fried cheese, sweet plantains, and homemade corn tortillas is a breakfast plate you must indulge in.

Arroz con…

Rice is a staple food in Costa Rica and served at most meals. One mouthwatering meal made with rice is arroz con pollo/camarones/vegetables/Marsico's (chicken/shrimp/vegetables/seafood). The rice is mixed with annatto (which is similar to saffron) to make yellow rice, and vegetables like peas, carrots, bell peppers, and celery are diced and cooked in. Then, of course, whatever "con" you decided on is thrown in the mix. This dish is quite simple, but incredibly flavorful.

Arroz con whatever you want

Chifrijo

Chifrijo is a compact dish that is usually served in bars. It is a bowl of rice and beans topped with fried pork meat or fried pork skins and topped with avocado, Pico de Gallo, chimichurri, and lime. There are few things that go better with an ice-cold Pilsen than a cup of chifrijo. Often this dish is accompanied by homemade tortilla chips or plantain chips. Every bit will make you smile.

Beer and chifrijo are a match made in heaven

Chicharrones

Chicharrones are something you should absolutely try, but maybe only once during your visit. Chicharrones are a very popular snack that are usually served at fiestas, family gatherings, bars, and any other type of celebration in Costa Rica. They are nothing short of scrumptious, but tip the fat and cholesterol scale. Chicharrones are fried pork rinds. It is so well-loved in Costa Rica that there is even an annual Chicharrones Fair in Puriscal to celebrate and serve up mass quantities of the delectable dish.

Definitely another favorite of mine, every Latin America country will have their own version of chicharrones.

Sopa negra

Not all places in Costa Rica are hot. In elevated zones or in the Central Valley temperatures can be quite moderate and sometimes even chilly. It is in these places that a bowl of sopa negra will taste its best. Sopa engram is traditional black bean SOUp. This is also Costa Rica's answer chicken noodle SOUp and served when people are sick. Sopa negra is typically served with two hard boiled eggs, a cup of rice, and a side of corn tortillas. A warming dish that is good for the SOUl.

Sopa Marsico's

Sopa Marsico's is a tomato-based SOUp that is packed with fresh seafood. The best place to order this SOUp is in a coastal town on the Pacific. Usually there is squid, shrimp, clams, mussels, pieces of white fish, and sometimes vegetables in this savory dish. This SOUp is a delicious taste of the ocean.

Pipa fria

While this is not technically a food unless you eat the inside – which is also highly recommended – a pipa fria is a must-have when on the coast. A pipa fria is a cold coconut which are usually sold on the streets or on the beach for between $1 and $2. There will be a man or a woman with a cooler filled with iced pipa frias, with the coconuts opened on the spot. This incredibly hydrating and refreshing beverage is the perfect midday revitalizer.

BELICE

When you think about Belize, your first thoughts don't usually remind you about the food in Belize.

Your first thoughts are usually about the glorious Belize Blue Hole, the Great Barrier Reef, the remnants of the vast Maya Empire dotting the landscape, the jolly Belizean faces and the pristine rainforests and nature reserves we are home to.

Belizean cuisine reflects the country's multiethnic population and rich history. When you blend all the diverse ingredients starting from the early Maya settlement through to the pirate past, the British settlers, the vibrant African influences, the attempted Spanish conquest, the Mennonite farming communities and the more recent influx of many other cultures, you have a recipe for something very, very special!

Foods that originated thousands of years ago are still served every day in Belize.

Tamale is a perfect example, having its origin in the earliest Maya cuisine, as does the finger-licking-good Cochinita Pibil style of cooking pork meat. This cochinita pibil is a skinned pig, marinated with strong acidic citrus juice, colored and flavored with annatto seed, wrapped in plantain leaves and buried underground overnight for a slow-roast.

Barbecue got its start with Buccaneers, whose name comes from buccan, an Arawak word for smoking meat, an occupation pirates busied themselves with while on shore or traded to keep a supply of meat aboard their vessels. So, it is said then, that our Belizean barbecues are a throwback to the days of pirates standing around the cooking meat drinking ale or rum and swapping stories. Cool like the Caribbean breeze!

Not much has changed either! Arawak cooking, combined with African influences, also survives today through Garifuna cooking. Meals such as the sere, fufu, cassava bread and hut hold their own place in the Belizean culinary honor roll.

The Spanish influences are apparent in much of our spices.

The British palate brings us a taste for bread, the styles of beer (we're thinking Belikin beer of course), cheeses and other staples.

The list of culinary influences is far too long to list here, but you get the idea. The term "melting pot" extends to the kitchen as much as to the people and cultures of Belize.

Rice and Beans

Top-Belize-Food-Rice-and-Beans

This Belizean staple is without a doubt the most abundant meal in Belize. From north to SOUth, east to west and out on the cayes, you won't go anywhere without coming across rice and beans. Every location, indeed, every family has its own variation, but all start with the basics – rice and RK, Red Kidney beans. Cook will then add more or less recados (an achiote based flavoring and coloring agent) and other spices, some coconut milk or none, and they can be moist or drier. However prepared, a meal without rice and beans is truly like a Belizean day without sunshine.

2. Stew Chicken

Top-Belize-Food-Stew-Chicken

The perfect plate mate to rice and beans, stew chicken is another ever-present dish that arrives on the table in any number of subtle variations. As its best, it is a sublime mix of spices and melt-in-the-mouth tender chicken, and at its worst it's not bad at all. Served with rice and beans and a scoop of Belizean potato salad, stew chicken (and its cousins stew pork and beef) makes for a filling and tasty meal any time of the day.

3. Tamale

Top-Belize-Food-Tamale

Dating back well before the time of Christ, this Maya staple also comes in many guises, from straight out of the pot to wood smoked and are delicious hot or cold. A variety of fillings, often with but not limited to chicken or pork, make up the center of a cornmeal roll which is wrapped in corn husks and steamed or boiled into something magical. While many people may be familiar with the Mexican version served in restaurants north of the border, the Belizean tamales are the real deal; virtually unchanged for thousands of years and just as delicious today as they were when gracing the tablets of both the Maya royalty and the humblest of homes.

4. Ceviche

Top-Belize-Food-Ceviche

This is another dish that goes back a long, long way! Simply, the seafood is marinated in lime juice with onions, garlic, habanero peppers and other ingredients and allowed to sit for a while. The complexity comes with the individual touch of each cook, and that can make a huge difference. With the Caribbean and Belize Great Barrier Reef attracting a huge variety of fish and home to a wide assortment of shellfish, ordering ceviche in Belize is always a good bet.

WHY BECOME A CHEF?

Why would anyone want to work 16 hours a week? Why would anyone want to work 80 hours a week? Why would anyone want to be in a hot, steamy kitchen, on your feet all day? Why would anyone work every holiday, every weekend?

These are just some of the questions I can come out with at the moment.
I have been in the business for over 30 years, and the only thing I can say to you, we do it for the love and passion that we feel for kitchens, and this is the number one reason, if you are thinking about working in a kitchen to make

money, find something else to do, the money is not enough for all the stress we take.

We all hear that old saying, in life you are what you do, there is not a day that goes by in any chef's kitchen, that you always try to be better than the day before.

Working in kitchens is addicting, it takes a special kind of people to do what we do.

Me personally, I used to say that I would never work in kitchens, for the simple fact that I hated my father, my father was a Chef and I did not want to be like him, I work in a thousand jobs before I worked in kitchens, and I got my ass fire after 3 months in every single job.

When I took my first job in a restaurant, I did it as I had worked in restaurants my whole life, it came very naturally, as if was in my genes.

I started from the bottom and worked my way all of ways to the top. If you ask me, that's the best way to do things, going from washing dishes all the way to become the head Chef. That's the old fashion way, and you will learn things that no school will teach you.

You will become a HANDS ON CHEF, you will learn how to work as a team, you will learn sympathy for others, when I had my business, I never had the heart to go home, and living my dishwasher buried with dishes to wash, I always grabbed an apron, and joined in to help him.

You will earn a tremendous amount of respect in your kitchen, working that way, at the same time, you are teaching your crew, no one is better than anyone, one stays everyone stays.

Since I started working in restaurants, I never really did anything else for a living, well, not until I got older and I got involved with import export business, the reason for that was due to a bad back, after being on my feet for so many years, it finally said stop, I had enough, three back surgeries later, I had to slow down a lot.

As I said before, working in kitchens is addicting, one of the best things about kitchens, is that you never stop learning, it goes on and on, so many different types of cuisine. I did them all, from Steak Houses, Seafood Places, Sushi to specialize in different types of cuisine, such as:

JEWISH

100% KOSHER

LATIN

SEAFOOD

ITALIAN

Often people ask me, what do you like to cook the most? Honestly, I love everything.

The fact of being in the kitchen is enough for me, being in a kitchen puts a smile on my face, from there you can ask for tacos or a very fancy gourmet meal, I would cook it gladly for you.

I always told my cooks, if you don't want to do something twice, do it right the first time. Be good at what you do is who you are.

If you don't feel like working, be honest with me, stay in bed, get some rest, but rest well, if you come to work in my kitchen, be awake, be ready for anything, and let's rock and roll.

I don't like half ass shit in my kitchen, if you don't give me your best, I will tell you to get that fuck out and god home, it's simple really.

Chefs don't beat around the bush, we can catch a lie a mile away, you better never to try to bullshit a Chef, most of us came from the st, we came from low income neighborhoods, we are very street-smart people.

Responsibility was taught to me at a very early age, I remember the first time I got drunk, my mother's first words were, you better not call in sick, you were man enough to go out and drink, and you will be man enough to suck it up and go to work.

We hate excuses in the kitchen, we hate crying babies, saying they are tired all the time. Complaining is something we do not do in kitchens.

If you went out to party the night before and got shit face, and slept one hour, the chef don't give it a shit, you better be in my kitchen on time, not only on time, a half hour before, so you can take a shit, wash your hands, drink your coffee and put your apron on.

I remember my younger years drinking at the bar up to 6 AM in the restaurant and say, shit, we open in 2 hours for brunch, let's get back to work.
Yes, the life of a chef is crazy, but unique.

Most of the crew in any kitchen come from low family income, some of the best Chefs come from a third world country, it is the type of work that is hands on, we get the say a lot of bad words, insult each other and have a beer together at the end of the day, get into a nasty fight, and become best friends after, yes, it takes a special kind of people to be in that business.

I wish it was not true but it is, the number of drugs that take place in a kitchen is unbelievable, the drinking gets way out of control, everything is abuse to the max in this type of business.

Chefs work a tremendous amount of hours, so cocaine was the SOUrce of energy for a lot of Chefs, people in the kitchen are usually drinkers as well, may be and just may be and of course it's just my humble opinion, you just had a long day of work, and you know that if you go home everyone in your house is already sleep, so what's the point on going home/? Minus well stay out and relax a little, take a little weight off your shoulders, get home whenever, take a nice hot shower, kiss the kids, the wife (if you still have one) and go to bed.

I think that people become Chefs because we enjoy pain, we love the pain to a certain extent, it is not fun having someone screaming right in your face when you start cooking.
The nice thing about working in kitchens is that you will always hear honesty from everyone, it's not like and office, when people talk behind your back and you walk by and they smile right in your face.
 If someone has something to say to you in a kitchen, they will go ahead and tell you right in your face, we don't like kiss asses either, and I think that a lot of those rules come from the streets, no one likes a rat, and I as I said previously, most of us come from very poor families.

It is the opportunity for any kid in the ghetto to become a Chef, is the opportunity to have a career and get pay rather then you paying to have a career, a Chef it's a very well respected career all over the world, the pay is well and the chance for growth it's amazing.

Despite me losing a wife, I absolutely love what I do, we wish it would be different, but the career of being a chef is demanding, and it is what it is.

If I had to complain about anything will be how the job has changed a little, with all the paperwork and all the shit that has nothing to do with cooking, chefs want to be in their kitchen, doing the things we love, which is cooking, not doing inventory, not doing schedules, not doing forecasting etc., but it is what it is.

In Mexico, there are plenty of good Chefs here, it is sad that they do not make good money, just like every third world country, anything that is hands on gets pay shit, that is why I keep advising young Chefs in Mexico to get out of Mexico and go to work in different countries, we have too many people wanting to do the same thing.

In the United States, things are different, the economy is better and most of the kids have a legitimate choice on what they want to do for the rest of their life, the sad thing is that if you ask most kids in the US in their mid-20s what they want to do with their lives, they will tell you I DON'T KNOW YET.

In Europe, it's a combination of both, the economy is not bad, but kids have at least a clue on what they want to do in their lives, which is always a good thing, to know what you want, to know what you want your future to be, your future always will be the result of your actions today, it's a very simple equation in life, not knowing what you want it's not going to give you a good future, is just simple math.

THE CRAZY ONES, THE ADDICTS, THE DRAMA QUEENS

Yes, we have all kinds of Chefs out there, we have the ones that are truthfully crazy, getting into fights all the time, restraining orders, kids everywhere, fucking anything that moves.

These are the type of guys that have an excuse for everything, these guys are the ones that blame everyone else for their mistakes, these are the guys who love to intimidate people for no reason, immigrants, low self-esteem people, insecure people etc., the question is how did these guys got to be Chefs.

The answer to that is easy, these guys are nothing but good line cooks, and the guy that promoted them was the owner of the restaurant in order to save money, Chefs? NOT AT ALL

The difference between a Chef and a line cook it's easy, Chefs are creative and live cook's follow orders and recipes.

So when an owner promotes a really good line cook to so call Chef, it works most of the time, for a little while, the cook will follow the menu he know for a good year and then what/ the reality for the restaurant owner will hit him like a bucket of ice cold water, in many cases the restaurant owner replaces the guy with another good line cook, in which case this line cook decides to get creative and you end up eating something like FRIED ROMAINE on a salad, WTF, what happens next, the restaurant closes and goes out of business, just for the simple fact that the owner wanted to save a few bucks, it is not worth it at all, it is always good to have a good Chef representing your menu, when I say good, I mean guys that have a lot of respect for their own name, their reputation, they will not fuck up their name for anyone, and there for, you will always get the best food in return.

The addicts, a lot of these guys are actually very good at what they do, the only problem is that they cannot function without being under the influence of something, alcohol is the most common one but not the only one, I would say cocaine is second, pills in third place, and now these days they have all kinds of new shit.

And weed of course, that goes without mention it, that just become normal along the way.

It is amazing, I have seen a lot of Chefs, high on cocaine and kick ass on a busy night, to do over 400 dinners and not even one complains, take their coke away, and you will have every dish come back to the kitchen.

It's the same thing for pills and all the other shit, except alcohol, in my opinion, alcohol is the worse drug there is, and its legal everywhere, I have seen more people do stupid shit under the influence of alcohol than any other drug, alcohol is very dangerous.

I am not saying any drug is good, but back in my day I would much rather do a couple of lines of coke then drink and drive.

The Drama Queens, oh god, I hate that type, everything is a big damn deal, they will drown in a glass of water, or make a big deal out of everything, those are the ones that won't even get their hands dirty, but will criticize you as if they can do it better than you, no one is better than them, never satisfied, they will never tell you how much of a good job everyone is doing.

Deep down, I think they are very insecure people, yes, I will be the first one to admit, we are strict, discipline, but putting someone down for your own amusement it's just wrong, putting someone down, so you can make yourself better it's absolutely wrong.

A drama queen, his uniform will always be impeccable, not even one dirty spot on them (they really prefer to keep their hands clean).

These guys will always have the nice cars, I had also nice cars, the difference was, my car always smells like food, I was always working, but a Drama Queen chef's car will always smell nice.

Something about a Drama Queen Chef I never liked, almost as if they were always trying too hard to show the world that they were nice people, it's almost that for them is all about the image than the food they cook, a Drama Queen Chef is always on your ass, asking how your food was, did you like it? What do you think? They are a pain in the ass, always looking for approval from everyone.

A lot of the Drama Queen Chefs leave with mom still, a lot of these guys went to school to become a Chef.

A lot of trophies for just participating and not doing a goddamn thing, you know the ones I am talking about?

A lot of these Chefs, end up working in homes, as personal Chefs of someone, working on yachts etc...

IMMIGRANTS IN THE KITCHEN

In every kitchen in America, 90 percent of the kitchen staff are immigrants, a very simple reason for that is that no one wants to work these number of hours, for the kind of pay that is being offered.

As I mentioned before, most people want to work 9to5, weekend off, regular vacations and all that bullshit.

A Mexican for example, the last thing on his mind will be the 401K plan you got to offer, or what type of health benefits you have available.

Yes, many restaurants explode the shit of immigrants, a lot of these immigrants do not mind, due to the amount of money they can send home, as long as they can build a home, send money to their children and send their kids to school, if they can do that, they will be happy without having a health insurance or a 401K plan for themselves.

Mexicans definitely are the ones dominating the kitchens, we do have other immigrants in kitchens, when it comes to immigrants in the USA, we can compare it to watching a movie of people being in Jail, in prison, everyone stays with their own race, it has nothing to do with being races, it's just tribal.

That's how most immigrants survive in the US, they stick together and help each other out, a lot of these guys leave all together in one apartment, everything they do they do it together, that is the only they can survive, in a country where they do not speak the language.

If you go to Chinatown, all the Chinese restaurants will have only Chinese cooks in their kitchens, if you go to a Ukrainian area, same things go on, and on and on it goes.

Without all immigrants in the kitchens, the restaurant business would not be what it is today, a lot of people work very hard so you can have a good meal, every-time you go out.

In my case, my right hand was a kid from Guerrero Mexico, he ended up being my Sue Chef, his name was Felipe.

When I first met Felipe, I asked him to give me five years of his life to help me build my business, and after five years, I was personality going to drive him home, when the five years went by, I drove him home, all the way from

Boston, Ma to Mexico Guerrero, he showed me his house, and said, this house is thanks to you, I said no Felipe, you earned this house on your own with all your hard work in the US, I tossed him the keys of Cherokee, and he said really? I said yes, it's yours, thank you for everything, we hugged and said our goodbyes, great guy Felipe.

That is a very typical story for a lot of immigrants in our kitchens in the US, the same thing goes around for the Russians, Cubans, Mexicans, Dominicans, etc.

Amid the clinking of glasses and low hum of diners' chatter, a waiter carries a salad bowl through a restaurant. This is not just a bowl of greens—these spinach leaves and romaine hearts represent a vast network of labor: from farmers planting the seeds and farm workers harvesting the greens, to drivers trucking them across state lines, and kitchen staff washing them, and many layers in between.

Immigrants are deeply involved in this complex journey from seed to plate. They are an essential link in the chain of our food system, and are an indelible part of rural America, contributing to the economic and cultural fabric of these communities. It's hard to picture our food system without them.

We have a big understanding with immigrants in the US, somehow, we are under the impression that they do not want to pay taxes, or become legal, or become citizens, or to enter the country legally.

Trust me when I tell you, they want to do all of the above, but the US government makes it almost impossible for them to do that.

Going to an American Embassy to ask for a visa, it is almost impossible, hell, I am an American and it took 32 requests for me to let me into my embassy (I live in México).

So, Imagine how hard it is if you are a Mexican, if you are lucky enough to get an appointment, the requirements for you to get a visa are impossible, you need to own property, in most cases they ask you to have a spouse, kids, a good bank account. The point being is, if you had all that, why would go and work in the US.

If we offered some kind of working visa in which they can be allowed to pay taxes.

May be a year or two-year visa? That would work for everyone, no one wants to be illegal, no one wants to cross fences and risk their lives.

There are better ways, other countries do not have this problem, Canada for example is one of these countries.

PERSONAL LIFE AS A CHEF

Zero, yes that's right, next to nothing, as I said before, our personal lives are reduced next to nothing, we do not get to spend a lot of time for our kids, taking our wife out for dinner in a Friday night is definitely out of the question.

Not spending the time with my kids when they were little, is what hurts me the most as an adult now.

I used to kiss my kids goodbye early in the morning, and goodnight late at night, I saw them on Sunday mornings, if I was lucky.

I always hope that was ex-wife would be more understandable, and never ask for a divorce, because I met her as a waitress.

I was wrong, of course she got tired after a while, anyone would, she is only human.
A couple of years later, I understood why it had to be rough for her to go to funerals without me, to go to weddings without me, I apologized for all that, she said that the funny thing was, that for years that went by, people would still think I was married, just for the simple reason that I was never there, people were so used to not seeing me around, so they assumed she was married after years of the divorce.

When it comes to friends, the only friends I had were my co-workers, the people I had around me, working next to me.

It's not that I did not want to have friends, I just did it have the time to socialize.

The only people I knew outside my work were my barber, my mechanic and my bartender.
Again, Chefs don't have many friends, but is not by choice, if you ever get to hang out with a

Chef, you will have the time of your life, we are fun people, we like to smile and shoot the shit.

- No Chef wants to get divorce, what would they want to divorce the woman they love, the woman they picked to be with for the rest of their lives, when years go by as you being a Chef, you will become nothing but a friend to your wife, you will become a roommate, or if you are lucky maybe a friend with benefits.

Love needs
-. work, you can't just expect it to be there every time you get home, staying in a relationship for a long time, requires a lot of work.

A DAY IN THE LIFE OF A CHEF

Early Morning

After first arriving at the restaurant, a chef must immediately begin to take inventory of all food and beverages. Produce deliveries often arrive in the morning, and it's the chef's responsibility to be sure that all fruits and vegetables are fresh. Likewise, the chef should check the rest of the inventory to make sure all food, beverages and condiments are being used before the expiration date.

Midmorning

Kitchen staff usually begin to arrive a short while after the chef does. This is the time when work should commence on any dishes that take longer to cook or can be prepared ahead of time, such as SOUps or desserts. Because a chef is usually also the supervisor of all employees who work in the kitchen, she also needs to make sure that every worker arrives on time. If she's short on staff, the chef should immediately begin making arrangements for additional workers to fill in if possible.

Midday

The lunch crowd typically begins to arrive around 11:30 a.m., and it's then that the chef's full attention must be devoted to how his staff is performing in the kitchen. It may be necessary for the chef to provide advice or instruction to staff members. It's equally common for the chef to pitch in and help in whatever area of the kitchen may be lagging behind.

Early Afternoon

After the lunch rush is over, a chef and her staff have time to take a lunch break of their own. Kitchen personnel usually stay at the restaurant and eat their midday meal together, often sampling potential new additions to the menu.

This is also the time of day when beverage distributors typically make their deliveries. It is the chef's responsibility to make sure that the delivery includes exactly those items that were ordered, in the proper quantities.

Late Afternoon

The chef supervises his kitchen staff as they prepare for the dinner crowd. This often involves making sauces, chopping and slicing vegetables and beginning to cook any meat that may take a long period of time to prepare, such as roasts or baked poultry.

Early Evening

The dinner crowd arrives in early evening, and this is most often the busiest time of day. Usually beginning around 6:00 p.m. and lasting until 9:00 or 10:00 that night, the dinner rush involves a great deal of activity in the kitchen, all of which must be supervised and coordinated by the chef. A chef's duties during this time of day can be compared to a conductor leading an orchestra.

Late Night

While kitchen employees are cleaning up, the chef takes the time to plan and review his menu for tomorrow. Now is also often the time for placing beverage and produce orders for the following day.

This type of life can go on and on for up to seven days at times, I remember working up to a year and a half one time, without a day off.

But yet, is what we love to do.

DRUGS IN THE KITCHEN

After more than 43 years in the hospitality industry, I am continually surprised to read about the problem of drug-taking among chefs. All staff in hotels are under pressure, and yet we never hear of housekeepers, sommeliers or receptionists resorting to stimulants in a big way.

Only recently young chef Philip Alford, of Lime Wood country house hotel, sadly died from a suspected heroin overdose. Michael Quinn, the first-ever British head chef at London's Ritz hotel, almost lost everything, including his life, through alcohol abuse. He has since founded the Ark Foundation and now does all he can to warn youngsters about the stresses of hotel work and the dangers of alcohol and drugs.

Why do chefs more than any other members of staff resort to stimulants to get them through the day? They're mainly behind the scenes and it is the waiters, receptionists and management that get the customers' complaints. If a diner is unhappy with the food, it is the waiter or waitress that hears about it - not the chef, hiding in the kitchen.

In my career, seven out of every 10 staff I have fired have been chefs. They can be some of the most difficult and demanding of employees, and often behave as if they own the hotel. When I bought my first hotel, it was not long before I sacked all four chefs and I have sacked even more since then, either because I have been unhappy with their attitude or they were uncomfortable with the high service standards that I expect from them.

I believe a lot of the bad attitude from chefs stems from the fact that they do not deal directly with the customer. Many works in their own little kingdom where they rule the roost.

In my hotel I involve my head chef, Michael Titherington, with the customers as much as possible. He will go through menus with them when functions are arranged, make suggestions and give them food tastings, so that he can make the event special for them.

If we've had a big lunch or dinner, I will always bring Michael out at the end of the meal and introduce him, so that guests can see the chef responsible for the food they have just eaten, and he is always applauded. This is important. I like my chefs to feel involved.

Maybe the key to this problem is simply to make chefs feel appreciated, rather than isolated below stairs in the kitchen.

Substance Abuse Amongst Chefs

I love *Hell's Kitchen* and *Kitchen Nightmares*, two Fox shows hosted by Gordon Ramsay, OBE, a British celebrity chef and a very strong personality. Watching this season of *Hell's Kitchen* reminded me of the stress and rigors that chefs in training regularly undergo. And something rarely mentioned on these shows — substance and alcohol abuse amongst student chefs.

While on internship in New York, I had the pleasure of serving at the local county department of mental hygiene (yes, mental health is like your teeth — you need to floss your brain regularly to keep it clean!). In one of my rotations there, I had the pleasure of seeing a few clients who were attending the prestigious **Culinary Institute of America**. This is one of the premier chef schools in America, and if you're ever in Hyde Park, New York, you should definitely make reservations at one of their restaurants (way ahead of time — they book up quickly).

One of the things related to me by some local mental health professionals was that a good many chefs-in-training grapples with the stress of the culinary training through excess — substance and alcohol abuse are commonplace. Surprisingly, I couldn't find a single study that examined substance abuse amongst chefs in culinary school. I know it's a niche area, but these are the same people who then go on to become a world-renowned chef. I think it would be interesting to see whether these issues resolve themselves after training is completed, or whether substance abuse continues on in the high-end, high-pressure kitchens. It would also be good to know that if this is a real problem, what schools can do better to help their students grapple with the stress of culinary studies. Word of mouth suggests it does go on, but that's highly unreliable and akin to gossip.

Violence and bullying are also commonplace amongst chefs working in high-end kitchens (Johns et. al., 1999). The stress to perform consistently and produce high-quality food of excellence day-in and day-out is overwhelming to most chefs. It seems reasonable to suppose that one way to deal with this stress or bullying is by turning to alcohol or substance abuse, if not during work hours, then definitely when the workday is all done (often in the wee hours of the morning).

These are not public health issues, since high-end kitchens do not stand low-quality output. Such chefs quickly are shown the door if their food preparation is not up to par (although, as our local public health board regularly shows, high-end restaurants seem just as susceptible to food poisoning incidents as the local McDonald's). But I do worry about the toll such jobs take on a person's humanity and sanity, all in the pursuit of excellence in cooking.

And so, while I sit there enjoying my episode of *Hell's Kitchen*, I can't help but wonder if I'm part of the problem, enjoying watching other people being bullied, harassed and threatened over the simple act of cooking.

Before you read any further, I must disclose that I have never—nor will ever—claim to be a psychologist or an expert on human behavior.

I'm simply an experienced club chef who has encountered individuals from many walks of life, and learned to develop and build relationships while gaining friendships. I also have developed the ability to observe and understand things on many different levels.

Below is my perspective on why I think many chefs suffer from addiction and depression.

First, we face a demanding schedule with a near-perfect performance standard. As a true chef, a "normal" day consists of 10-16 hours on our feet, sometimes more. We constantly multitask, plan ahead, problem-solve, and ensure each task is completed with the utmost attention to detail. We do all this while receiving feedback from irrational members and guests in highly variable and subjective situations.

Our work environment is usually crammed, loud, and hot. There's rarely any natural light. And we're constantly worried that our line cooks and dishwashers will show up and not find themselves in jail.

We develop a daily plan for the countless reservations we are about to cook for all while ensuring our labor, food cost and other budget line items are where they should be. And let's not forget that we are also ensuring orders for the next day are being placed and are accurate and that the multiple purveyors we work with are not going to short us or send us any sub-par products.

These are only some of the daily thoughts that go through our minds as we try to continuously improve ourselves as well as motivate our brigades to ensure each service is flawless.

So, when I ask myself, why is addiction so prevalent in our industry and why is the depression rate higher than most any other professions I can start to see some trends.

From the most obvious standpoint, we work long hours on our feet around type-A personalities. We look for an edge to help our creativity, or allow us to work long hours without slowing down. And we deal with members and guests who, as of recent thanks to the food network, have become experts on food and cooking.

But food is extremely subjective. And so, we face constant change to our visions and dishes. We pour countless hours into preparing and balancing each and every bit, just to have a customer modify the hell out of it or try to dissect each component instead of understanding that when the flavors and textures are eaten together, it is perfectly balanced—at least in our own mind's eye.

You all know this stress and anxiety. And nearly all of us know how to escape. Some days we need more of an escape than others, but each day is different. Most of us try to create a plan for the following day before we leave the club but, as most of us know, that plan rarely goes as intended. And on top of the plan, changing the number of tasks that are completed in a day's work are countless.

But every time we complete a task, we experience a small rush of dopamine. We feel good. In my very unprofessional opinion, I can only imagine the amount of dopamine our bodies produce throughout our day as we cross off tasks and move on to the next all while successfully completing a busy dinner service.

But what happens when we leave the kitchen and head home. The dopamine wears off. The multitasking subsides. The troubleshooting and problem-solving is put on hold. But we are still riding the high of an exhausting and exhilarating day. Is this the reason we head to the bar for "just a few beers" or participate in illegal drug use or head to the casino to blow off some steam? Are we trying to continue that dopamine rush? And what happens when we can't? Do we crash?

In my humble opinion, over the past ten years or so, chefs have done a far better job of understanding the importance of the work-life balance. We have substituted unhealthy coping habits with exercise, yoga, running and other activities that stimulate our brains and bodies to help us deal with the countless pressures we take on. We are better equipped to approach our days with an open mindset, a philosophy to effect change and develop cultures in our kitchens that are team driven and positive.

Even so, addiction and depression are still very serious issues that many of us struggle with. I encourage you to take a minute and evaluate your own mindset. Find healthy escapes and lean on people who you trust to carry you through the rough spots. Mental health is a serious subject. Please don't take it lightly.

EXOTIC FOOD

Exotic food to you, not to exotic to the people who eat it every day, a bear burger in Africa is normal for a native, but for you, will be exotic as hell.

Caviar, exotic for most people, and just a normal thing for a Russian to eat, so what is exotic? it's just something that you are not used to eat on a daily basis, something that is not part of your day to day diet perhaps.

I have had the pleasure to eat interesting plates, grilled snake, turtle egg SOUp, bear burger, alligator sushi, dog tacos, yes dog tacos, not by choice but of way, I was told what I had after I ate them, the meat had this distinctive flavor, very lean, in china dog food is a normal dish, in Mexico there are a lot of street taco places where you will eat dog food without you even knowing what you are eating.

Dog is also a common dish in Spain, alone with horse meat.

In Chiapas Mexico, monkey in Mole, as a chef we are very curious people, but Monkey is where I draw the line.

They also have the Iguana end Pepian, very similar to an Iguana Stew.

A lot of these dishes may SOUnd disgusting to most people, but very normal to the natives.

Some other types of cuisines I like dude to the unusual ingredients at the Portuguese. They have dishes with very odd mix of ingredients, Carne Alentejana for example, (Pork and Clams), SOUnds nasty I know, but they have a way to make this dish, and it's just delicious, the Portuguese are masters on combining Seafood and meat together, most of these dishes will be served with potatoes tossed with piti, a local Portuguese spicy pepper.

You may consider eating a Camel exotic, when in fact in Jordan, it's just an everyday thing to do, so again, I ask you, what is EXOTIC FOOD?

It's my personal opinion that exotic does not actually exist, it's just a different way of cuisine on which you are not used to it.

WHY IS THERE ONLY A FEW WOMEN IN PROFESSIONAL KITCHEN

I would say the main reason for that, is not that guys cook better than women, as I said before, cooking is an art, an expression, love, so being a man or being a woman has nothing to do with being a good Chef of not. I think the reason for not having enough women in our kitchens are;

1. LONG HOURS

2. HEAVY LIFTING

3. ROUGH WORK ENVIRONMENT

4. MALE DOMINATED WORLD

5. LONG HOURS

It's not every woman's dream to be working seven days a week, or not to want to see her kids, or not to see their husbands.

Being a female Chef, has to be one of the most difficult things someone can do, they have to be mothers, wives, and Chefs and all at the same time.

I take my hat off to all the women that work in kitchens.

HEAVY LIFTING

Myself, I have three back surgeries, do to all the bad lifting, all catering jobs we did, Catering jobs are the worse for your back, there is a lot of lifting involved, you can't have any excuses, you can't say, or that's too heavy for me, or let the men do it, it does not work like that.

ROUGH ENVIRONMENT

Chefs are not necessarily executive professionals when it comes to speak proper in a kitchen; most women in the world are delicate and sensitive to our kind of language.

As a woman in a kitchen, I think you would have had to grow up in the middle of 10 brothers and be thought as nails, and be able to take it.

MALE DOMINATED

Yes, a lot of macho and testosterone in kitchens all over the world, it's a man's world, and a woman has to work twice as hard in order to prove herself in a kitchen.

Fair? Not at all, but again, I stop asking what is fair or not fair in this world a long time ago.

Life is definitely not fair, most Chef will always tell you, if you are going to cry, please do it in the walk-in and take the broom with you so you can actually accomplish something while you there.

You will never get a lot of sympathy in any professional kitchen, we do not like crying babies, if attention is what you are looking for, a professional kitchen will be the wrong place to get it.

Remember, we try to do better and better every day, crying and bitching is not how we are going to accomplish anything.

DIFFERENT TYPE OF CHEFS

CATERING TYPE

PERSONAL TYPE

EXECUTIVE CHEF

HIGH END CHEF

CATERING CHEF

As I previously mentioned before, catering is rough, catering it's not an easy task, as a catering chef, you have to pre plan menus with your clients, a lot of these menus are customized menus.

The client will ask you for exotic things, that is what's fun about catering, you do not have face a boarding ass menu every day, every day or every job you will be challenged with a different type of food.

Customized menus, it's what sells when you do catering, it's as if you are their private Taylor, and you make this dish just for them.

When do you catering you face many different challenges, what if the truck breaks down? How about you get into an accident on the way there? How about your head CHEF does not show up the day of the event? A good caterer has many different plans in case of any of that happening.

Me personally, I always preferred to go to the site where I was going to cater the event the day before, to drop my equipment, and whatever other things I could have ready, in case of any emergency coming up, it's not if you are going to have an emergency, the real question is when are you going to have an emergency, its meant to happen, sooner or later.

Catering chefs that get ready at the last minute are idiots, a good chef will always be one step

ahead of time.

It is very similar to being in the military, always be ready and always be one step ahead of time, ALWAYS.

PERSONAL CHEF

This type of job is different, as a personal chef you have to know all your client's needs, such as, if he is a diabetic for example, any heart disease going on, is he trying to lose weight? Most of the time when someone requires a personal Chef its health reasons.

So, knowing all your client's needs, it is a most. Also, it won't hurt having a dietitian degree, so you can advise your client on what to eat and what not to eat, you will be surprised if I tell you that not even Doctors know a lot about diets.

As a personal Chef, their kitchen is your kitchen, you have to have a chat with them, that is no longer their kitchen, you will take it over as a professional, you will keep it clean, organized at all times, and with everything level with dates of the week.

As their personal Chef, you have to know every corner of that kitchen, being a personal Chef has a lot of responsibilities, so you have to be very careful with every decision you make.

Personal Chef, means you will become very personal with them, in some cases paperwork is necessary, so always be ready to sign confidentiality papers with your clients.

EXECUTIVE CHEF

A very common title to all the Chefs working in Restaurants all over the world, an Executive Chef is responsible for the overall of the Restaurant.

Things from inventory, purchasing, schedules, cooking, keeping a kitchen clean and organized, it's all part of the everyday of an Executive Chef.

A restaurant owner, always has to make sure to have a good Executive Chef in his kitchen, most restaurants close and go out of business for not having a good Chef in their kitchens.

A lazy Chef can cost you and it can cost you a lot, if you do not cut the problem on time it will cost you the whole restaurant.

A good Executive Chef, will always be concern about his image, his name, his reputation, to them, reputation is everything, people in restaurants are not the forgiving type, you can serve someone 100 times and everything is fantastic, but fuck up once, and they will not come back to your restaurant.

HIGH END CHEF

In order to become a High End Chef, you will need a lot of experience, you need to have been all of the above, your clients will have a lot of money and they can have anything they want at any time, your clients will be demanding as hell, just because the simple fact that they can be.

I had cooked for the Rolling's Stones, and plenty of celebrities, we are talking about clients that have been all over the world, they know what good food is, and they will demand nothing but the best from you.

As a High-End Chef, you will have to be creative with every dish, even if you are serving something as simple as Filet Mignon, you have to find a way for that to taste different to make look exotic, to combine that with something out of the world.

Your clients will always want something out of you that they cannot get around their town, if Pasta Puttanesca is what they want, they would not have a High-End Chef, they will just go around the corner, and fine and nearest Italian restaurant and order it.

NOTE;

If you are not in a position to hire a High-End Chef, they are very expensive, date one, (I am kidding) but it works.

INTERVIEW BY BOSTON NEWSPAPER

Chef Omar Sagastume has served Hillary Clinton and Sting, Tony Bennett and the Rolling Stones, but he's also happy to cater any event, from a small family party to a large wedding.

"We're very flexible. We'll work with any budget," Sagastume said. "You can call me for a party of 10 up to 1,000 people. We're actually doing 2,000 people for Boston College."

Sagastume works with each client to determine what the budget is and what the client wants.

"Every party is different. Most caterers hand you a book of menus [to choose from]," he said. "We sit down with you and figure out: what is your favorite food? What are you picturing for the day of the event?"

And he works with any budget.

"If you say, 'I got $500, what can you do?' I come up with two different options," SAGASTUME said. "Who am I to tell you what to have and how much to spend? If I am going to spend $5,000 on my son's bar mitzvah, I want to sit down and talk with [the caterer]."

One of his wealthier clients regularly calls him for events that include people such as singer Tony Bennett. But that doesn't mean the client wants to throw money at a caterer, SAGASTUME said.

"He knows he can get the same quality [at a better price from Cardoos]," SAGASTUME said. "The whole idea is we can cook for an average person all the way to Ernie Boch."

While Cardoos often focuses on Middle Eastern foods, there is no limit to the variety, from Italian to barbecue to whatever the client wants, he said.

"Our biggest thing is customizing whatever you want," he said.

SAGASTUME has the experience to do just that. Along with his duties with Cardoos, he owns the Mayan Café in Grafton, which offers elaborate Sunday brunches, as well as lunch, breakfast and coffee in a comfortable setting. The café also hosts monthly dinners with live music. With more than 20 years' experience, SAGASTUME is able to find a menu to suit every event, budget and taste with personal service, high-quality gourmet fare and professionally-trained wait staff and bartenders, as well as professional event planners.

Cardoos works in many venues, including the Sumner House in Shrewsbury and Mechanics Hall in

Worcester. But, SAGASTUME isn't limited to large, showy locations. Cardoos can provide a professional, elegant, gourmet event in any setting, from a backyard barbecue to a cocktail reception in a home.

"I want people to know that we cater every function," SAGASTUME said.

About Sting: he loves French-pressed coffee, according to SAGASTUME. And Ron Woods of the Rolling Stones is a big sushi fan. Serving Sting was a very special experience, SAGASTUME said, since as a child in Guatemala, before he even learned English, he loved the British singer's music. When he told Sting he was a fan, the musician invited him to chat.

His experience with Hillary Rodham Clinton was different. She wasn't eating the sandwich he had prepared, SAGASTUME said. Although he usually doesn't interrupt, he asked her if everything was all right.

"She said, 'Yes, [the food] is fine. President Regan just died,'" SAGASTUME recalled. "So, I knew before everyone [about the former president's death]."

Cafe Mayan, Where the Love of Coffee

Runs in the Family

Omar Sagastume, founder of Cafe Mayan, is no stranger to the world of coffee. As a child growing up in Guatemala, his grandfather taught him all about the family business of growing coffee beans. He taught Omar the importance of selecting the highest quality beans and heating them to the optimal temperature to extract the beans' highest quality of flavor

Cafe Mayan is more than just a gourmet food and beverage establishment. We cater to a diverse group of customers, from business people to college students. We serve the finest dishes and drinks during private parties, public or corporate events. With WineOnline.ca professionals buy alcohol online for your private events and parties and let us create delicious beverages! Also, Cafe Mayan is the best place for coffee and beer lovers. And if you are a big fan of delicious craft beer, we advise you to visit craft beer bar in Los Angeles, to discover an impressive assortment of beer on tap.

Cafe Mayan is the perfect place to meet old friends and make new ones, or simply to relax and let the world go by.

COMPETITIONS

The Millbury Bicentennial Committee has announced the names of the three local chefs who will contend for the title of "Millbury Bicentennial Chef 2011" at the third annual Millbury Bicentennial Committee Wine Tasting and Culinary Competition. The event will be held on Saturday, October 29, from 7:00 p.m. to 9:00 p.m. at Asa Waters Mansion.

Chefs will include last year's culinary competition winners and Scales restaurant's new owners Chefs Dean and Shari Della Ventura, who will prepare roast pork tenderloin with apple chutney and honey glaze. A chef for more than 27 years, Chef Dean's love for cooking began in his grandmother's kitchen when he was just a little boy. He has served as an executive chef throughout New York and Massachusetts. Shari has been serving customers for more than 25 years and has truly mastered the art of customer satisfaction. Together they complement each other perfectly, and their talents even landed them on national TV in NBC's restaurant competition reality show, "The Chopping Block." This once-in-a-lifetime opportunity allowed them to work with world-renowned master chef Marco Pierre White.

Also competing will be Chef June Weiner, the 2009 culinary competition winner, who will prepare a caramelized onion tart with poppy seeds, bacon, and dates along with a roasted garlic and almond SOUp shooter. Chef June has tinkered in the kitchen since childhood, and her delectable dishes have satisfied the most discriminating tastes. Her culinary expertise ranges from informal intimate events to large scale occasions. She currently hosts a cooking show called "The Casual Gourmet" on local cable television in Ashland, which is filmed in her own kitchen.

The final competitor will be Chef Omar Sagastume, owner of Cardoos Gourmet Caterers, who will prepare seared breast of chicken served with caramelized apple and onion jam. Chef Omar has more than 20 years of culinary experience, and has catered events that included these notable political figures as guests: former Massachusetts Governor Mitt Romney, Boston Mayor Thomas Menino, Secretary of State Hillary Clinton, former Vice President Dick Cheney, and former Florida Governor Jeb Bush. In the entertainment arena, singers Mariah Carey and Cher as well as members of the legendary rock band The Rolling Stones have enjoyed Chef Omar's exquisite culinary creations. Chef Omar has cultivated his cooking expertise by collaborating with some of the top caterers in the Boston area, and has further enhanced his abilities through multi-cultural experiences. His culinary palette includes flavors from Portuguese, French, Latin, and Middle Eastern cuisine.

Guests attending the event will be able to taste a tapas-sized portion of each chef's signature creation, and then vote by secret ballot to determine the winner. In addition to the culinary competition,

Lenny's Liquors will again provide dozens of varieties of wine and beer for sampling. Several raffles will also be held that night.

FUNDRAISERS

Local chefs and television personalities were featured at the Natick VNA's annual Fresh Taste fundraiser held at Elm Bank in Wellesley.

On Thursday, June 16th, "A Fresh Taste: An Evening with Local Chefs Showcasing Fresh Ingredients" was held at the Elm Bank Reservation in Wellesley with nearly 300 in attendance. The evening featured local Boston area celebrity chefs including Gregory Talmont of The Sherborn Inn, Jim Solomon of The Fireplace, Omar Sagastume of Cardoos Gourmet Caterers, and more. All event proceeds benefited the Natick Visiting Nurse Association a nonprofit home health care agency headquartered in Natick serving 20 MetroWest Boston towns.

EXPORTING COFFEE FROM GUATEMALA

As a Chef I had a lot of fun exporting coffee

Company Introduction

we are a coffee plantation in Guatemala that offers grower-direct pricing on 100% Arabica SHB coffee beans. We can offer: Raw green beans, roasted to spec, private labeling, etc.

} Order Credit Report

Company Basic Information

- - Company Name MultiCafe de Guatemala
- - Location Boynton Beach,
- - Business Type Manufacturer
- - Year Established 1990
- - Employees Total 51 - 100
- - Annual Revenue More than 100,000,000

- - Website-
- - EC21 Storefrontus03712698.en.ec21.com
-
- - Selling Categories **Agriculture** > Beans
- - **Keyword Coffee**, beans, green beans, raw

Contact Information

- - **Address**200 Knuth Rd., suite 238B Boynton Beach, FL
- - **Country/Region** United States
- - **Phone**+1 - 978 - 3840111
- - **Fax**
- - **Contact** Omar SAGASTUME

CEOOMARSAGASTUMEATGMAIL.COM